Siren's Tears

Katherine Balla

BookLeaf Publishing

Presentation by *BookLeaf Publishing*

Web: www.bookleafpub.com

E-mail: info@bookleafpub.com

ISBN: 9789357690270

First edition 2022

ACKNOWLEDGEMENT

I have a heart full of gratitude for my family, Sarah and Miranda for encouraging me to brave the stormy seas of doubt to put forth my best fin forward and sing my songs for the public.

PREFACE

You've heard the tale of merfolk time and time again... But how can you know their intent if you never sat by the water's edge and listened to the words they sang.

Siren Tears Never Fall

Silence
In the air
Rising waves
Engulfing the
Nightly ships

Tales
Echoing chaos
Around mermaids
Raising fear
Ships sail o'er the horizon

Never again to be seen
Every story begins again
Varies from land to land
Every man goes missing
Rarely sees a mermaid alive

Floating
Alone
Lost in the sea's
Labyrinth

Truly Me

Drowning in a sea
of endless wonder.
When you call to me-
do I follow?

Your words of poison-
promise salvation.
But how can one save
someone broken like me?

For I'm a mermaid-
one with the Ocean,
wild and free
and you just want to tame me.

Do I drown in words
or drown in pity?
Do I change to comply
or abandon our dreams
to remain:
truly me.

The In-Between

I cannot breathe down below
nor walk on land as thee.
Some place between is where I'll find
my rightful place to be.

No land nor sea do claim me,
no easy way to find
my place among the Siren's call,
nor dance along to the band.

Why can't the world just get along?
For neither right nor wrong.
The voices sharp like broken shards
and blades so sharp to end them.

To neither race do I belong,
since equals cannot be.
Where differences fight day and night-
that's no place for me.

Lonely But Not Broken

They say you can be anything
when you find your place in the world.
So I decided to use my voice
and be the Siren I'm meant to be.

They didn't tell me I'd be lonely,
but that's how I'm supposed to be.
To guard my heart
in a distant place beneath the sea.

But I'm meant to cry these Siren tears
to keep from falling in love.
I'd rather have a lonely voice
than be a broken-hearted fool.

Fragmented Voices

Swimming through the darkness
I can't seem to find escape
following the empty void
in search of your gentle guiding light.

I hear the echoes through the water
attempting to get close to you,
but every time I search
there's just no end in sight.

Endless circles of "I love you"
"Come find me"
and "let's try one more time"
and I'm the one left deep, alone, behind.

Gentle Love, I can no longer
find the courage to fight again
I bid you "Adieu"
and hope the Ocean guides you home.

Find yourself at peace
away from down below
for falling for a mermaid
hurts more than you could know.

Slow Dance Serenade

Have you ever danced with a mermaid?
So broken and unfound.
The taunting voice scratching the air.
The broken scales littering the water's surface.

There is no joyful music
down where she is found.
When you grow up in a fortress,
it's hard to see the world around.

She's been alone for so long.
She doesn't understand how
you can want to hold her close
and dance to the music in your heart.

Be patient, young sailor.
She can give you her world.
If you hold her close
and show her how to dance.

Teach her how to walk,
one step in front of the other.
Free her from her solitude
and she'll dance with you forever.

Distorted

When I look at you I see warm.
When I look at you I see cold.
Your head is in the clouds.
Your head is under the water.
You live a life of reality.
You live a life of fantasy.
A sword in hand.
A piercing voice.
Your legs always guide you.
Your fins will propel you.
In the end:
In the end:
I will always love you,
I will always love you,

For being my distorted flame.

Reflecting Love

Looking up from under the surface,
I see the same pain reflected back.
The same pain in a different face.
A face I once knew.
You know I'm a creature of the deep,
showing you what you fear most.
The frightfulness within yourself.
Afraid of committing to the monster
who has shown you kindness and pain
one too many times before.
You fear giving into the reflection below you,
dragging the monsters within you out to play.
Leaving you alone to join me down below,
where pain and pleasure mix.

Prized Possessions

Mermaids guard their treasure,
keep it hidden from you and I.
You pour over your maps,
point your compass due North.
At the end of the day,
your hands in the sand,
not a piece of gold to be found.
Legend will tell you,
it's the best treasure around.
You'll travel the world for years,
empty handed as the day you started.
What you will fail to learn,
is the mermaids' biggest treasure
are their hearts buried deep
inside their chests.

Monsters

History is told by the valiant heroes,
at least that's what they say.
But listen closely to the Sirens' silent songs-
that's where you'll find your way.

Sailors come and sailors go,
on ships and boats so grandiose.
But when their ships lay broken all ashore,
it's our songs that are to blame.

If it's our singing that's the cause,
what of their songs in response?
Their nets that they throw to capture us,
their spears that they throw to pierce us.

Because we are shiny and different,
such a sight to own and behold.
Each day makes them richer,
as we remain a trophy for the taking.

But blame us they do,
for we are the monsters down below.
As we perish in cages on land,
or mounted dead up on the wall.

Take a look in the mirror and you will find,
the creature you've created,
stares back at you victorious-
while the siren remains defeated.

Rest Your Secrets With Me

Send overboard your dead to me,
let them rest below the sea.
Down in Davy Jones' Locker
rests others just like them.
Let me care for your departed men.
Let me guide them towards eternal life.
Let the secrets you buried emerge
from the dead men's mouths.
For on the Ocean's floor,
I'll travel far and wide,
in search of getting justice.
Both men and women alike-
destined to rest in the locker
for the rest of eternity.

Imprisoned in Paradise

You say these islands
Are the most beautiful.
Yet all I see and hear
Are my sisters gone missing.
The tears on the planks,
Rotting away the wood beneath
Your unworthy feet.
For an Island so rich
Needs mermaids to thrive.
Where once were many,
Now lay barren down below
on the Ocean floor
Our resting place above ground.
Scales, tails, shells and tears
Scattered everywhere.
Beautiful island-
Terrifying graveyard.

Memories of Freedom

Isn't it grand?
A life adrift at sea.
A mermaid's life-
so free.

Just basking in the sun,
signing songs,
splashing tails in the sea-
so free.

Drawing men towards us,
trying to get their best view,
a rare beauty and sight-
so free.

Greedy men with their greedy minds,
armed with guns and ropes,
entrapping us for their own pleasures.
Leaving us longing to be once again-

so free.

Fractured Image

It's a trickling tear
running down a mermaid's cheek.

It's the tired muscles
moving the faded scaled tail.

It's the ringing song
echoing deep from within her breast.

What we know from history
is mermaids cannot shatter.

They only grow stronger
more deadly
with every heartbreak.

Crowning

You carved out my twin,
affixed her to your prow.
Tempting the Ocean
to bring you your crown.
You plunder the helpless.
You take what's now yours.
You think you're so brave,
the lawless pirate on the Sea.
Yet do you stand a chance?
When you go to the water's edge,
on the other side of the horizon
are the Sea's crowning daughters.
The sirens ready with tridents in hand
for you will meet your match.
Give back to the sirens,
make peace with your deeds.
Let them take care of the travelers.
that you buried in their Sea.

Mermaid's Lament

The ships do break
the ocean does shake
when the angry Siren calls.
The heartbreak of the scorned
will forever mourn.
The sky grows dark
and the air goes still
when the pained Siren wails.
Her tears will raise the ocean.
Who will mourn or note
when no Siren does sing
of a lost lover's song again?

Caged

No two people are alike,
but they'll always end the same.
You'll think about how to entice a mermaid
to the point you believe she's yours.

You will think you are charming,
a one of a kind man
who's going to show her
just how to enjoy the land.

You'll cage her at home
in a tank of clean water.
You'll visit her daily,
recounting your tales of pillaging her sea,
the home you took her from.

But one day she will grow bolder,
tired of being your pet.
She's been plotting and waiting
for you to come home.
She'll take you away to a cage down below.
She'll give you the courtesy you gave her.
She'll visit you too, she'll stay by your side
until you choke your last breath.

Embraced Mistakes

Pirates, sailors, sea traders and travelers-
they all fall the same.
No matter the title or status they claim,
all fair game to a mermaid's appeal.
With a voice of beauty
and the image to match,
they just can't help themselves.
But take it too far and they'll bring you down
to their homes below
where you cannot breathe.
They will show their beauty comes for a price.
Their claws and bite and shark-like strength
will have your last breath begging for your life.
A trophy for them to claim.
Do not welcome their summons.
Turn your ship away in haste.
Avoid the beauty of the mermaid
or they'll be your last dying embrace.

Seafarer Storyteller

The undead sounds
ringing in the water,
raising the hair on arms
of unknowing travelers.
For the pain of anguish
knows no gender, race, nor realm.
Every soul knows of love
and can feel the highs and lows
echo through the universe.
When the storms grow dangerous,
know the power of a wounded woman.
When the calm waves still your ship,
know of love neverending.
In the in-betweens,
there is no need to worry
for you can guide your own ship,
your own story.
Your ship is not wrecked
and you will find your voice
and the waters will still
in your own time.

The Final Judgement

Crimson tides
and salty tears.
The sailors out to sea.
The biting waves gnash
against the Captain's hull-
bringing them to me.

Crimson tides
and salty tears.
The sailors kneel before me
awaiting final sentence.
Praying for their families-
willing to make a deal.

Crimson tides
and salty tears.
I finally get to be
the thing they fear-
the monster they claim
down below the deep sea.

Crimson tides
and salty tears.
Pay respects newly departed.
They took their chance

and so did I,
heeding not to their mercy.

Crimson tides
and salty tears.
The echoes of screams fill the air.
As the storm starts brewing,
a quick flash and all is swallowed
while the Sirens start to rise.

Crimson tides
and salty tears.
A new dawn does appear.

A Debt to Pay

One thousand souls- a debt to pay,
to bring my loved one back.
I swore to bring the Ocean men-
who had to pay their way.

But weary am I-
to slay the men,
while loved ones await return.
Sitting on polished balconies daily,
watching the moon dance with the sun.

To no avail,
their sailor won't return,
Just ten more souls to go...
no....

        my love
        is
        finally

        free.